FIND OUT ABOUT **FOOD**
CONOCE LA **COMIDA**

MILK AND CHEESE/LECHE Y QUESO

by/por Tea Benduhn

Reading consultant/Consultora de lectura: Susan Nations, M.Ed.,
author, literacy coach, consultant in literacy development/
autora, tutora de alfabetización, consultora de desarrollo de la lectura

WEEKLY READER
PUBLISHING

Please visit our web site at: www.garethstevens.com
For a free color catalog describing our list of high-quality books,
call 1-800-542-2595 (USA) or 1-800-387-3178 (Canada).

Library of Congress Cataloging-in-Publication Data available upon request from publisher.

ISBN: 978-0-8368-8457-9 (lib. bdg.)
ISBN: 978-0-8368-8464-7 (softcover)

This edition first published in 2008 by
Weekly Reader® Books
An imprint of Gareth Stevens Publishing
1 Reader's Digest Road
Pleasantville, NY 10570-7000 USA

Copyright © 2008 by Gareth Stevens, Inc.

Managing editor: Valerie J. Weber
Art direction: Tammy West
Graphic designer: Scott Krall
Picture research: Diane Laska-Swanke
Photographer: Gregg Andersen
Production: Jessica Yanke
Spanish translation: Tatiana Acosta and Guillermo Gutiérrez

Printed in the United States of America

1 2 3 4 5 6 7 8 9 11 10 09 08 07

Note to Educators and Parents

Reading is such an exciting adventure for young children! They are beginning to integrate their oral language skills with written language. To encourage children along the path to early literacy, books must be colorful, engaging, and interesting; they should invite the young reader to explore both the print and the pictures.

The *Find Out About Food* series is designed to help children understand the value of good nutrition and eating to stay healthy. In each book, young readers will learn how their favorite foods — and possibly some new ones — fit into a balanced diet.

Each book is specially designed to support the young reader in the reading process. The familiar topics are appealing to young children and invite them to read — and re-read — again and again. The full-color photographs and enhanced text further support the student during the reading process.

In addition to serving as wonderful picture books in schools, libraries, homes, and other places where children learn to love reading, these books are specifically intended to be read within an instructional guided reading group. This small group setting allows beginning readers to work with a fluent adult model as they make meaning from the text. After children develop fluency with the text and content, the book can be read independently. Children and adults alike will find these books supportive, engaging, and fun!

— Susan Nations, M.Ed., author, literacy coach, and consultant in literacy development

---

Nota para los maestros y los padres

¡Leer es una aventura tan emocionante para los niños pequeños! A esta edad están comenzando a integrar su manejo del lenguaje oral con el lenguaje escrito. Para animar a los niños en el camino de la lectura incipiente, los libros deben ser coloridos, estimulantes e interesantes; deben invitar a los jóvenes lectores a explorar la letra impresa y las ilustraciones.

Conoce la comida es una colección diseñada para ayudar a los jóvenes lectores a entender la importancia de una nutrición apropiada y el papel de la alimentación en la salud. En cada libro, los jóvenes lectores aprenderán de qué forma sus alimentos favoritos —y posiblemente algunos nuevos— pueden formar parte de una dieta balanceada.

Cada libro está especialmente diseñado para ayudar a los jóvenes lectores en el proceso de lectura. Los temas familiares llaman la atención de los niños y los invitan a leer una y otra vez. Las fotografías a todo color y el tamaño de la letra ayudan aún más al estudiante en el proceso de lectura.

Además de servir como maravillosos libros ilustrados en escuelas, bibliotecas, hogares y otros lugares donde los niños aprenden a amar la lectura, estos libros han sido especialmente concebidos para ser leídos en un grupo de lectura guiada. Este contexto permite que los lectores incipientes trabajen con un adulto que domina la lectura mientras van determinando el significado del texto. Una vez que los niños dominan el texto y el contenido, el libro puede ser leído de manera independiente. ¡Estos libros les resultarán útiles, estimulantes y divertidos a niños y a adultos por igual!

— Susan Nations, M.Ed., autora, tutora de alfabetización, consultora de desarrollo de la lectura

Do you like to drink milk? Do you like to eat cheese? Cheese is a **milk product**. It is made from milk.

¿Te gusta beber leche? ¿Te gusta comer queso? El queso es un **producto lácteo**. Se hace con leche.

Milk is part of the **food pyramid**. The six colored bands on the food pyramid stand for types of foods. Make smart choices. Eat these foods and **exercise** every day.

La leche y el queso son parte de la **pirámide alimentaria**. Cada una de las seis franjas de colores de la pirámide representa un tipo de alimento. Elige de forma inteligente. Consume estos alimentos y haz **ejercicio** todos los días.

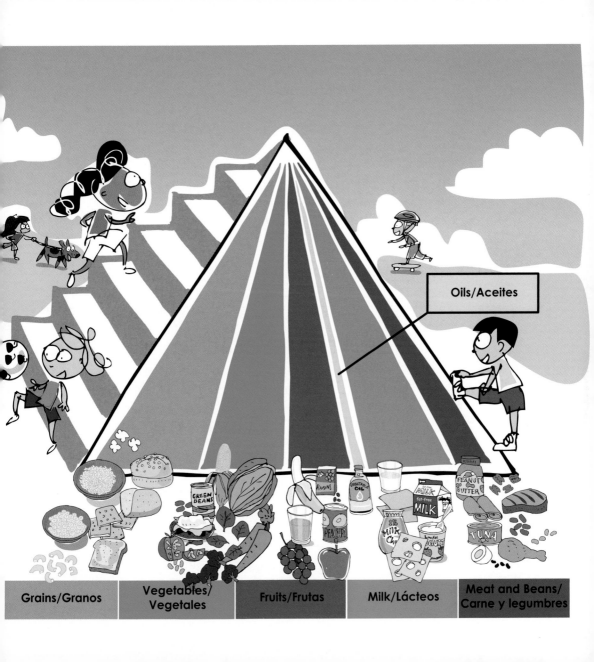

The blue band stands for milk and milk products. It is a wide band. You should have lots of milk or cheese every day.

La franja azul representa la leche y los productos lácteos. Es una franja ancha. A diario, debes consumir mucha leche o mucho queso.

Milk and cheese are good for you.
They build your bones and keep
them strong. They make your teeth
strong, too.

Consumir leche y queso es bueno.
Estos alimentos ayudan a formar
y a fortalecer tus huesos. También
contribuyen a la salud de tus dientes.

Some kinds of milk are better for you than others. **Fat-free** and **low-fat** milk are best. Milk that is low in fat helps you stay **healthy**.

Algunos tipos de leche son mejores para ti que otros. Las leches **descremada** y **semi-descremada** son las mejores. La leche con poca grasa te ayuda a estar **saludable**.

Most milk in the store comes from cows.
Milk comes from other animals, too.
People drink goat's milk. They even
drink milk from sheep!

La mayoría de la leche que venden
las tiendas viene de las vacas.
También hay leche de otros animales.
Hay gente que toma leche de cabra.
¡Algunas personas beben incluso leche
de oveja!

15

What types of cheese do you like?
Do you like cheddar cheese or
American cheese?

¿Qué tipos de queso te gustan?
¿Te gusta el queso cheddar o
el americano?

17

What other milk products do you eat? Do you eat ice cream or cottage cheese? Ice cream and cottage cheese are milk products.

¿Qué otros productos lácteos consumes? ¿Comes helado o requesón? El helado y el requesón son productos lácteos.

19

Yogurt is made from milk, too. Yogurt is a good snack. Can you think of other snacks made from milk?

El **yogur** se hace con leche. El yogur es un buen tentempié. ¿Se te ocurren otros tentempiés hechos con leche?

Glossary/Glosario

fat-free — describing a food that does not have fat in it

food pyramid — the drawing that shows six colored bands that stand for the six different food groups people should eat every day

healthy — strong and free from illness

low-fat — describing a food that is low in fat

milk product — a food made from milk

yogurt — a thick, creamy food made from milk

----

descremado — tipo de alimento que no tiene grasa

pirámide alimentaria — dibujo que muestra seis franjas de colores que representan seis grupos diferentes de alimentos que las personas deben comer a diario

producto lácteo — alimento hecho con leche

saludable — fuerte y sin enfermedades

semi-descremado — tipo de alimento que tiene poca grasa

yogur — alimento denso y cremoso hecho con leche

22

For More Information/Más información

Books/Libros

Los productos lácteos. Los grupos de alimentos (series). Robin Nelson (Lerner Publications)

The Milk Group. Eating Healthy with MyPyramid (series). Mari C. Schuh (Capstone Press)

Milk, Yogurt, and Cheese. Blastoff! Readers: The New Food Guide Pyramid (series). Emily K. Green (Bellwether Media)

Web Sites/Páginas Web

My Pyramid for Kids
mypyramid.gov/kids/index.html
Click on links to play a game and learn more at the government's Web site about the food pyramid.

Index/Índice

About the Author/Información sobre la autora

Tea Benduhn writes and edits books for children and teens. She lives in the beautiful state of Wisconsin with her husband and two cats. The walls of their home are lined with bookshelves filled with books. Tea says, "I read every day. It is more fun than watching television!"

Tea Benduhn escribe y corrige libros para niños y adolescentes. Vive en el bello estado de Wisconsin con su esposo y dos gatos. Las paredes de su casa están cubiertas de estanterías con libros. Tea dice: "Leo todos los días. ¡Es más divertido que ver televisión!".